VOLUME 1

Encouraging Women
of the Bible

Special thanks to:

Dan Kane – Editor

Jen McGee – Editor

Heather Cusumano – Cover Design

Grace Courter – Video Editor

The authors and publication team have attempted to give proper credit to quotes and thoughts that are not original with the authors. It is not our intent to claim originality with any quote or thought that could not readily be tied to an original source.

ISBN: 9798357982797

Printed in the United States of America

Table of Contents

Dedication

The aged women likewise, that they be in behaviour as becometh holiness...- Titus 2:3a

Aunt June, I love you!

Thank you for being such an incredible source of encouragement to me throughout my life. Some of my favorite childhood memories include you! Your giving spirit, steadfast love for Jesus, and your passion to live a holy life for Him has inspired me in more ways than you will ever know. I will always be thankful for the gift of friendship God has given to me in you. Thank you for everything!

Love,
Charity

Introduction

Digging Deeper!

Don't you love learning something new about your favorite Bible character or someone in Scripture that you thought you knew almost everything about?

For many years Encouragement From Women has shared daily devotionals written by women who love Jesus and study His Word. These women have shared their heartaches and the healing power that only comes through knowing and resting in Jesus. Daily devotionals written by others who've experienced the power of God in their life can be an incredible encouragement to the lives of the reader. But here at EFW, we know that God did not intend for us to only find encouragement through others experiences in God's Word, but through digging deeper into His precious Word for ourselves. That is why we have designed this Bible study.

We know that it can be difficult to study out the Scriptures alone during busy seasons of life so we created this study as a companion guide to help you along the way. Along with this guide you can view the sessions that accompany each of the studies.

To access the video sessions from a computer, visit **encouragementfromwomen.com**. Hover over the tab that says "Resources". Tap on the "Encouraging Women of the Bible Sessions" tab. Enter the password **EFW2023**. Click on the video of your choice and enjoy!

To access the video sessions from a phone or tablet visit **encouragementfromwomen.com**. Tap the three small lines in the upper right hand corner then tap the tab, "Resources", scroll down to the bottom of the page, tap on "Encouraging Women of the Bible Sessions" tab. Enter the password **EFW2023**. Click on the video of your choice and enjoy!

Before you dive right in, be sure to visit page 8 labeled "Group Leader Helps" to get the most out of your Bible study! Thanks so much for joining us!

Be encouraged!
Charity

Meet the Contributors

Charity Berkey

Charity Berkey is the founder of Encouragement From Women (EFW) where they provide daily biblical encouragement and resources for women around the globe. Charity resides in her hometown of Las Vegas where she and her husband, Neal, have served on staff at Liberty Baptist Church for the past eighteen years. Though she loves serving in various ministries such as hosting the podcast *Teis Talks*, speaking at ladies events and authoring Christian resources, Charity's favorite calling continues to be that of wife to Neal and homeschool mom to their four children Tre, Cherish, Lincoln and Felicity. Connect with her on social media, Instagram: Charity Berkey, Facebook: Neal Charity Berkey.

Alana Brown

Alana is the Senior Pastor's wife at West Florida Baptist Church in Milton, Florida, where she serves with her husband and four children. She came to know Christ at an early age, grew up in ministry and feels a great desire to have real conversations about real life centered on the teachings and truths of God's Word. Being highly involved in the church and school ministry, she leads the ladies' ministry, mentors, counsels, teaches, and enjoys being a speaker to ladies of all ages. She loves theater, the beach, coffee, and most of all, shoes! Connect with her on social media, Facebook: Alana Brown (Stewart), Instagram: alanabrown06, or Email: abrown@westfloridabaptist.com.

Micah Maddox

Micah Maddox is a women's event speaker and author who loves to give a voice to hurting hearts. As a pastor's wife, mother of five, and foster mom, she writes and speaks to the ones who need encouragement. You can find her book, *Anchored In*, on Amazon. Connect with her on social media, Instagram: mrsmicah, or Facebook: Micah Maddox.

Meet the Contributors

Melody Holloway

Melody grew up in a pastor's home. She currently is serving as a school counselor at a K-8 charter school in AZ. She has had the pleasure of working with children and teens for over a decade in various capacities, including camp ministries. Currently, she is privileged to teach God's Word and co-lead the women's ministry at her church. When she's not coaching volleyball, she's scoping out the local coffee scene, hosting afternoon tea, FaceTiming her family, reading, or watching Perry Mason reruns.

Hollie Vaughn

Hollie is a wife, mother, friend, pastor's wife, writer, and speaker. She and her husband Dan have been happily married since 2003. They have been blessed with four children: Jesse, Jeffrey, Olivia, and Kamryn. In 2004 they planted Hope's Point Baptist Church in Weston, WV. Hollie spends much of her life investing in the lives of others in her church, community, as well as ministry wives across the country. She oversees the social media page, Ladies Prayer Advance and has written several devotional Bible study materials. She was a founding member of the social media ministry, Simply Edify. Aside from spending time with family, Hollie is passionate about thrifting and coffee. She owns and operates My Thrifty Mama alongside her mom and enjoys her signature lavender vanilla latte from The Coffeehouse which is operated by her church. You can follow their ministries on social media, Facebook: HopesPointBC, ladiesprayeradvance, simplyedify.

Donna Wilson

Donna is the wife of her college best friend, Donny Wilson. Together they have served at Lighthouse Baptist Church in Moreno Valley, California for 21 years where Donny serves as the lead pastor. They have four energetic children that she homeschools. Working on house projects, playing with dogs, singing random songs and traveling are just a few ways they enjoy their family time. Donna has a heart for ministry, whether it's putting together church events, speaking to ladies or having people in their home, she loves getting to use her talents for the Lord. On any given morning you will find Donna sitting with her dog, Mildred, working on Bible studies and sipping a hot cup of coffee made by her husband because she has yet to figure out the coffee maker.

Group Leader Helps
To ensure a successful small group experience, read the following information before beginning:

Group Preparation
Preparations for the Bible study are of utmost importance to ensure an enjoyable time for each member of the group. Choose a group facilitator – The group facilitator will be responsible for announcements, testing the video to assure it connects to your video source and choosing a time and place for each meeting as well as honoring the agreed-upon timeframe of the meeting. You will want to prepare discussion questions from the study notes provided in the daily studies.

Access Video Sessions
To access the video sessions from a computer visit **encouragementfromwomen.com**. Hover over the tab that says "Resources". Tap on the "Encouraging Women of the Bible Sessions" tab. Enter the password **EFW2023**. Click on the video of your choice and enjoy!

To access the video sessions from a phone or tablet visit **encouragementfromwomen.com**. Tap the three small lines in the upper right hand corner. Tap the tab "Resources". Scroll down to the bottom of the page, tap on "Encouraging Women of the Bible Sessions" tab. Enter the password **EFW2023**. Click on the video of your choice and enjoy!

Sample Suggested Schedule
6:00 pm – Facilitator welcomes and prays with the group
6:05 pm – Announce time for next group meeting and remind those who have yet to purchase a book where they can get one
6:10 pm – Watch video session
6:50 pm – Break up into small groups for discussion questions and prayer
7:00 pm – Dismissal
*Many groups add icebreaker games during the welcome time or provide beverages and snacks. This is all up to you and your group's desires.

Lesson Format
Each lesson begins with video session notes, an outline of the session's video teaching for group members to follow along. Each author has provided five consecutive days worth of study for at home use. Please encourage your group members to read through each study on their own.

Hannah
Finding Your Identity in God

ENCOURAGEMENT FROM WOMEN

Week 1 - Video Session Notes
GRACE ← Hannah: Finding Your Identity in God

Introduction:

Piniah — thinks better than others

I. Hannah Did The Next _Right_ **Thing.**

I Samuel 1: 6-7

And her adversary also provoked her sore, for to make her fret, because the Lord had shut up her womb. And as he did so year by year, when she went up to the house of the Lord, so she provoked her;

II. Hannah _Shared_ **Her Struggle.**

I Samuel 1: 7-12

Therefore she wept, and did not eat. Then said Elkanah her husband to her, Hannah, why weepest thou? and why eatest thou not? and why is thy heart grieved? am not I better to thee than ten sons? Now Hannah, she spake in her heart; only her lips moved, but her voice was not heard: therefore Eli thought she had been drunken. And Eli said unto her, How long wilt thou be drunken? put away thy wine from thee. And Hannah answered and said, No, my lord, I am a woman of a sorrowful spirit: I have drunk neither wine nor strong drink, but have poured out my soul before the Lord. Count not thine handmaid for a daughter of Belial: for out of the abundance of my complaint and grief have I spoken hitherto. Then Eli answered and said, Go in peace: and the God of Israel grant thee thy petition that thou hast asked of him. And she said, Let thine handmaid find grace in thy sight. So the woman went her way, and did eat, and her countenance was no more sad.

III. Hannah _Praised_ **God.**

True Apology
1. I am sorry
2. I was wrong
3. Please forgive me

11

I Samuel 1:24 – 28

And when she had weaned him, she took him up with her, with three bullocks, and one ephah of flour, and a bottle of wine, and brought him unto the house of the Lord in Shiloh: and the child was young. And they slew a bullock, and brought the child to Eli. And she said, Oh my lord, as thy soul liveth, my lord, I am the woman that stood by thee here, praying unto the Lord. For this child I prayed; and the Lord hath given me my petition which I asked of him: Therefore also I have lent him to the Lord; as long as he liveth he shall be lent to the Lord. And he worshipped the Lord there.

Conclusion:

_____

_____

_____

_____

Answers: *Right, Shared, Praised*

Daily Study - Day 1
Read 1 Samuel 1

Contentment is found in God alone. That is what the story of Hannah is all about. The book of 1 Samuel does not claim an author but most scholars believe that Samuel may have written the first 24 chapters, which is a biography of his life up until his death.

Some eleven hundred years before Jesus the Messiah was born, a young woman by the name of Hannah would become the mother of one of the most well known prophets of God, Samuel. Many barren women have found comfort in learning of Hannah. Knowing that Hannah petitioned God for a child and that God miraculously answered that request gives hope of a loving, personal, and prayer-answering God.

Similar to many modern-day romances, Hannah's story includes marriage. Hannah's husband, Elkanah was a Levite and therefore a direct descendent of Aaron the priest, Moses' big brother. The Levites didn't have any land of their own. The other tribes of Israel were instructed to provide land for the Levites (Numbers 35:2). This little family of Levites found themselves living in Ephrathite territory. Remarkably, the Ephrathites were the descendants of yet another great hero of the faith, Joseph.

Similar to many fictitious tales, Hannah's historical reality included a true to life villain, Peninnah. Peninnah was also the wife of Elkanah. Many scholars speculate that Hannah was the first wife of Elkanah but due to her lack of producing offspring, Elkanah chose the path of polygamy to produce a child of his own.

The entire first verse tells of Elkanah's life living as a descendent of men with a great legacy. The second verse shows the contrast of the lives of this husband and wife, depicting Hannah's torment. Hannah was married to a man who had two wives. The opposing wife Peninnah was blessed with multiple children. Hannah wanted nothing more than to have a child and yet, God shut up her womb.

These first few verses give us a look inside the beginning of Hannah's horror story and it only gets worse before it gets better. 1 Samuel gives a front row seat to the grief of a broken home, the faithfulness of an ever-loving Savior, and hope for true contentment. Only an omnipotent, all loving God could bring beauty from these ashes. Hannah's eternal love story will blossom as we observe her consistently doing the next right thing.

Study Questions

1. Paraphrase 1 Samuel 1

2. What are the emotions you think Hannah was feeling based on her circumstances?

   Sadness, bitter, anger, resentment

3. Have you experienced grief similar to Hannah's?

   Yes

4. Do you suppose our Savior has purpose for your pain?

   Yes

5. What characteristic of God stands out to you after rereading 1 Samuel 1?

   Grace and Love

Daily Study - Day 2
Read 1 Samuel 1:1-5

Times were tough. The land was filled with abundance yet there was a spiritual famine in the lives of God's people. Can you picture Hannah living during a time when many of the spiritual leaders in the land were living in opposition to God Almighty? Hophni and Phinehas were priests. They were the sons of Eli the priest. The Bible is very clear that both Hophni and Phinehas lived in opposition to the God of Israel (1 Samuel 2:12-17, 22-25). Not only were they well known for their thievery of the sacred sacrifices but for committing sexual sin with the female servants at the very door of the tabernacle of God.

Yearly Elkanah would take his entire family to Shiloh, the place of rest and the tabernacle, in order to sacrifice to the Lord. The great temple of the Lord that was later built in Jerusalem by Solomon had not been erected yet (1 Kings 6:1-10). You may notice in 1 Samuel 1:9 that the word "temple" is used simply as a dwelling place.

These sacrifices were most likely part of the peace offering, an offering of thanks unto Jehovah. The peace offering was the only offering in which worshipers offered part of the offering up to God and the rest was consumed by the worshipers in a meal (Leviticus 7:11-13, and 15).

In verses 4 and 5 of 1 Samuel 1, we get a picture of what this ritual looked like for a family. The head of the home, Elkanah, served each member of the family a portion or a part of the sacrifice for them to consume. Since the Bible mentions that Penninah had both sons and daughters we can assume there were 7 or more people feasting. Verse 5 specifically states that, *But unto Hannah he gave a worthy portion; for he loved Hannah.* It has often been taught that a "worthy portion" was equivalent to being a double portion, showing favoritism towards Hannah. Yet, many scholars share opposing views on what the original writer was expressing. Many insist that the worthy portion that was given was just one portion, enough for one, worthy of one. Even though he loved her, he only gave her one portion because God had not given her children for him to give more portions to. This was meant to be a beautiful time of thanksgiving and yet it only brought more sorrow to Hannah.

When spiritual leaders live in hypocrisy it can be detrimental to the church of God. Have you had a spiritual leader let you down? I'm sure we all have.

Maybe it was a moral failure such as Hophni and Phinehas or maybe it was something different, something more personal, intentionally directed at you. What we must remember is that just because some spiritual leader is living in hypocrisy, such a one does not represent all spiritual leaders. It can be depressing to think of all the sinful failures of different spiritual leaders, yet that should not be our focus. Hannah stood unwavering in her faith, through her struggle even when her spiritual leaders lacked integrity.

We see here that our God is personal! He deals with us as individuals. Hannah could have easily let her faith waver because of the difficult time she was experiencing. She could have turned from her faith due to the lack of integrity from her spiritual leaders, but she didn't. She remained grounded in her faith.

Study Questions

1. Have you had a spiritual leader let you down?

2. If so, how did that affect your faith?

3. We are all spiritual leaders to someone in some way. Are you living your life free of hypocrisy?

4. How have you seen God work individually in your life?

Daily Study - Day 3
Read 1 Samuel 1:6-7

Who is your Peninnah? Your adversary? Your rival?

Peninnah grieved Hannah so much so that the Bible says Peninnah provoked her *to make her fret*. The Hebrew word used here for fret is *ra'am* and it gives the idea of causing inward commotion that can result with an outward reaction such as a roaring or a thundering. Peninnah was purposefully causing deep grief and inward turmoil to Hannah's soul and the result was a thundering, roaring pain.

Do you have pain in your life right now? Hurt that no one knows about? Perhaps you have a Peninnah in your life. We see that the person who was causing so much grief in Hannah's life was someone who did religious acts (v. 7). Hannah's adversary, while on the way to worship at the tabernacle, filled the talking space with contempt, disputing, and evil speaking. The hypocrisy of Peninnah was hurtful and the contempt was constant. Yet in all of Hannah's roaring, inward turmoil, Hannah continued to do the next right thing.

There will be people in our lives who claim the name of Christ and yet they don't live for Him. We cannot allow someone else's hypocrisy to dictate or affect our relationship with the Lord in a negative way. Hannah, even in her pain, went up to the dwelling place of the LORD.

Are you in a place like Hannah? Scripture tells us she was in such depression that she stopped eating. Are you having a difficult time even participating in the everyday routines of life? Are the daily tasks of this life daunting to you right now? Can I encourage you to continue in the things of the Lord? In your turmoil, bring your requests to our Savior. **Continue to be faithful to your local church.** As we continue our study, we will see in the days to come that the Lord comforted Hannah when she was at the house of God.

Maybe your Peninnah attends your church, sings in the choir, or leads in ministry. Perhaps your adversary has been blessed the way you desire to be blessed. She may have everyone fooled into believing that she is living her life for the Lord, but you know the truth. Like Hannah, we must not let someone else's sin prevent us from doing what God has called us to do. We will stand before God for our own actions, not the actions of our adversaries, but also for our response to their actions.

During this extensive 14-mile journey with rugged terrain, I suppose there were at times a deafening silence between these two women. I imagine the silence being broken by a glance accompanied by a cutting comment from Peninnah such as, "If only God would give you a child!" Or perhaps Peninnah was more passive aggressive, "God has just overly blessed me with children! I love this time of year, going to worship and thank God for His provision of children! Hannah, what will you thank God for as you worship?"

Hannah's contentment could not be found in her circumstances. Her joy could not be found on her journey. Her happiness was not in her earthly relationships or happenstance. We will see tomorrow that God used these situations and more to bring Hannah closer to Him, the only One Who can bring eternal comfort, joy and contentment.

Study Questions

1. Who is your adversary?

2. Have you allowed the actions of your adversary to prevent you from serving our Savior?

3. Have you tried to find contentment in anything other than our Savior?

4. What is God currently calling you to do? Are you finding it difficult because of your circumstances?

5. What actionable steps can you take to do the next right thing in your life?

Daily Study - Day 4
Read 1 Samuel 1:8-16

The wrong kind of love. Have you ever had someone try to show you love but it backfired?

When my future husband and I were first dating, he didn't have much experience in the romance department. One night while sitting in my parents living room, my boyfriend, Neal, looked over me at me and said, "Charity, loving you is like…" he paused. While he paused I imagined he would say something like, "Loving you is like joy I have never known!" or "Loving you is like the sunrise after a stormy night!" or even, "Loving you is like the cherry on top of an ice cream Sunday." But that's not what was said. He continued, "Charity, loving you…loving you is like…falling down the stairs without the pain!" Fifteen years later and I'm still not exactly sure where he was going with that, and we still laugh about it to this day.

We can only imagine what Elkanah was thinking when he said to his wife who was in the depths of despair, *…why is thy heart grieved? am not I better to thee than ten sons?* If ever a man said the wrong thing at the wrong time, it was here.

Often we seek comfort from those who care, yet cannot fill the void that only our loving God can fill. We must first and foremost bring our hurt to The Healer. We see Hannah doing exactly that in the continuing verses.

I envision the exciting celebration of thanksgiving going on at the tabernacle, and the hustle and bustle of large families eagerly waiting to give their sacrifice of thanksgiving to the Lord. And yet, Hannah we see in verse 10 is in bitterness of soul. This is the same wording we see in the book of Ruth when Naomi returns to her home of Bethel after her husband and two adult sons have died. She tells everyone to call her, Mara, which means "bitter" (Ruth 1:20-21).

Hannah's pain was as deep as someone who had lost a husband and two children, but Hannah took that bitterness to our beloved Father.

Have you ever been in a large gathering where someone was doing something that they shouldn't? Someone in a large audience speaks out when only the keynote speaker should be talking? It's socially awkward isn't it? It's awkward for everyone.

While the rest of the Israelites were at the tabernacle worshiping the Lord, Hannah was pouring her heart out to the Lord. The Bible indicates that she spoke to the Lord in her heart, but that she also mouthed the words, but no voice spoke. When Eli the priest noticed her, his first assumption was an accusation in the form of a question, *How long wilt thou be drunken?* I can only imagine the awkwardness of that moment.

Accusations are typically the worst way to approach anyone living in sin. We are commanded to address sin, but there is a right and a wrong way to go about it. Asking non-accusing questions is one of our best ways to address someone who may be hurting and living in sin.

Because Hannah had her heart in the right place, her response was the proper response. Many people have the wrong response when they are accused. When Jesus was accused, the Bible says, *"He opened not His mouth."* (Isaiah 53:7) (Matthew 27:14). Sometimes, the right response is no response. In this case, Hannah was able to first pour out her heart, her distress, and her bitterness to the Lord. She then was able to share her struggle with a godly counselor, the priest, Samuel.

Study Questions

1. Have you been falsely accused? How was your response?

2. Read Matthew 27 and summarize how Jesus responded when He was falsely accused.

3. Have you experienced the deep pain that brings about the bitterness of soul that Hannah was experiencing? Have you taken that bitterness to our Savior?

Daily Study - Day 5
Read 1 Samuel 1:17-28, 2:1-10

Identity. We all want four things in life: salvation, security, safety and significance. Our significance really says, "This is who I am and what I have done." In all reality, our significance resides in our identity. Our world says we can find our identity in our gender, our nationality, our feelings, our social status, or even our job title. Yet, as a child of God, we know that we cannot find significance apart from our Savior! **It doesn't matter who you are until you know Whose you are!**

Hannah's situation didn't get much better. God did give her a baby, in fact, he gave her three more sons and two daughters (Samuel 2:21)! But her adversary was still there and Hannah fulfilled her vow to God by giving her first-born son back to Him. Hannah's contentment was coming from knowing God more and knowing who she was in Him. She was the handmade of the One true King (1 Samuel 1:11). Her identity resided in knowing that she belonged to the Father. She finally recognized who she was in HIM!

The question is often posed, "Why do bad things happen to good people?" It's a legitimate question. In the case of Job, the Old Testament example of a man who lost everything, God not only **allowed** Job's pain and suffering, God actually **suggests** Job's name to Satan (Job 1:8). Job was known as an upright man and yet he was experiencing trials, not because of anything wrong he had done, but because of Satanic attack.

Another well-known Bible example who had some terrible tribulation was Jonah (Jonah 1:17). Rotting alive in the belly of a fish is one of the worst things anyone could ever imagine. Jonah was a well-known prophet of God who had a godly reputation, yet he fled in disobedience to God. In Jonah's case, he brought his bad experience on himself. Often people are experiencing trials because they are in defiance to God's Word, even though they are children of God.

Hannah's circumstance was different. She was actively serving the Lord and pursuing Him. The Lord not only **allowed** her pain, but the Lord **caused** it. Why would a loving God prevent His own daughter from having children? Why would He withhold such a precious gift, the gift she desired more than anything? Can I suggest that God prevented Hannah from getting pregnant so that she could find her true contentment and identity in Him?

In the Scripture reading today we see that God eventually answered, "yes," and gave Hannah a child. But the receiving of a child, a "yes" answer to her pleading prayers was not what changed Hannah from a woman of bitterness to a woman of praise.

Please catch this! The last six words of verse 18 state that after she went to the tabernacle (doing the next right thing), she pleaded her cause to the Lord, shared her struggle with Eli (found wise godly counsel), and it was only then that *her countenance was no more sad.*

Hannah was **not** pregnant when her countenance changed! She did **not** have the promise of a baby. Then what changed? What created contentment from the inside that showed on the outside?

She had brought her bitterness to the Savior and in doing so she was reminded of whom she was in God. She belonged to Him!

Maybe like Hannah, you desire something that God has withheld from you. The Bible assures us that *no good thing will he withhold from them that walk uprightly*, (Psalm 84:11). This is not a promise to receive anything that we want. This is an assurance that if we are living our lives in accordance with His ways, we can be steadfast in knowing that He will provide what is best for our lives, what is good for our circumstances. He knows what is good for us and as our loving Father He will do what is right towards us (Matthew 7:11).

Just as Hannah found her true joy and contentment in the only One who could provide it, so can we find our true joy and contentment in knowing whom we are in Christ.

In closing we should remember that in the beginning of our story Hannah identified as an adversary of Penninah. 1 Samuel 1:6 uses the word "fret," *ra'am* in Hebrew. As you recall the original meaning of the word gave the idea of roaring and thundering. The very last verse where we hear the words of Hannah, once she knows her identity in Jehovah God, she states, *The adversaries of the LORD shall be broken to pieces; out of heaven shall he thunder upon them.*

The Hebrew word used for thunder here is the exact same word that we find in in 1 Samuel 1:6.

Hannah not only found out who she was in God, but she learned that He could take away her fret, her thundering, her roaring. Sometimes we make people our enemy who truly aren't our enemy but are being used by our Enemy. She recognizes that God will take care of His adversaries, His thundering, His roaring is the only kind of *ra'am* that is truly beneficial. As you meditate on Hannah's prayer of thanksgiving, notice everything she points out about the God she has truly come to know. It's ALL about Him.

Study Questions

1. Take some time to read over and meditate on Hannah's prayer in 1 Samuel 2:1-11. Write your own prayer of thanksgiving to God.

2. Have you found your significance in your Savior? Have you trusted Jesus Christ as your Savior? If not, please go to the back of this book to page 104, entitled, "You Can Know You're Going to Heaven!"

3. Have you lost sight of who you are in the sight of God? Look up the passages below and share who God's Word says you are in Him. Ephesians 2:10; Psalm 139:14; 2 Corinthians 6:18

4. We come to the Scriptures, not to find who we are, that is just a byproduct of Bible study. We study to know the mind of God. We learn so that we can know Him better. What can we learn about our Savior through the verses above?

Mary and Martha
The Balancing Act of Life

Week 2 - Video Session Notes
Mary and Martha: The Balancing Act of Life

Introduction:

_____
_____
_____
_____

I. _____ Hurrying.

But Martha was cumbered about much serving, and came to him, and said, Lord, dost thou not care that my sister hath left me to serve alone? bid her therefore that she help me. Luke 10:40

II. _____ Down.

And she had a sister called Mary, which also sat at Jesus' feet, and heard his word. Luke 10:39

III. _____ In.

But one thing is needful: and Mary hath chosen that good part, which shall not be taken away from her. Luke 10:42

There they made him a supper; and Martha served: but Lazarus was one of them that sat at the table with him. Then took Mary a pound of ointment of spikenard, very costly, and anointed the feet of Jesus, and wiped his feet with her hair: and the house was filled with the odour of the ointment. John 12:2-3

Conclusion:

_____
_____
_____
_____

Answers: *Stop Hurrying, Sit Down, Lean In*

Daily Study - Day 1
Read Luke 10:38-42

God-given relationships matter. Looking at the relationship between Mary and Martha goes deeper than their blood kinship. Their relationship was ordained of the Lord to encourage one another in truth.

Mary and Martha were serving together on this beautiful day when their friend and Savior arrived. They were excited! Although both had different reactions to His coming, we can see in the scope of this story, the story that God took time to record in His eternal Word, the value of both sisters.

We are not told in Scripture the birth order of this sibling crew, but we can take some educated guesses. Mary and Martha were not the only two children; they also were sisters to their brother Lazarus. We know this because in John 11:1 it mentions Lazarus and his relationship to his sisters. We will assume due to personality that Martha is the oldest, Mary is the middle and Lazarus is, perhaps, the youngest. This birth order might help us further understand the reactions to this situation.

Because of Mary and Martha's strong reaction to Lazarus's death in John 11, we can see that these siblings had a love for one another. Mary and Martha have no husbands listed in Scripture and according to studies, these ladies ran their own household. I am not sure about you, but if I choose to live with someone, it would mean that I like them. I emphasize this because often we can take a snippet of Scripture and conclude an "it was always this way" attitude.

Mary and Martha loved one another as siblings, as roommates, as friends. I am sure they had their disagreements, as we see in this example, but that was not what defined them. Because we are human, we often fail. We fail in our actions, in our words, and often, in our relationships. Let us not use our weaknesses as an excuse, but as a reminder that when someone in a relationship fails us, we are capable of the very same thing. We want grace in our failures, and in turn we should extend grace to others.

If it were not for Mary and Martha's relationship, we would not have this beautiful example of how we should react to Jesus being in our very presence. Look at your relationships today. See the value, and realize that God ordains them for a greater purpose.

Study Questions

1. What is the purpose of relationships?

2. Who is your strongest earthly relationship?

3. Why do you think God has placed close relationships in your life?

4. How can you add value to these relationships?

5. Is there a broken relationship that needs to be restored through forgiveness?

Daily Study - Day 2
Read Luke 10:38-39; John 11:20

God-given personalities are a gift. But why was I created with...?! You fill in the blank. I am sure that we have all uttered these words at some time or many times in our lives. It usually follows a big mess that we have made due to the misuse of our personality. If these traits are a gift from God, then why do they seem to get us into trouble?

I am certain Martha had the same thoughts the day she was lovingly corrected by her Savior. Why didn't I just put the mixing bowl down? Martha's personality seems to be pragmatic. I mean, Jesus, God Himself, was coming to her house! And, no doubt, He was probably arriving with other travelers. I am not sure about you, but I am with Martha. Put out the fine china, the food, the fanfare. After all, these guys were hungry! They were not going to be neglected on my watch and, apparently, not on Martha's. There would certainly be time for sitting around and talking later.

Mary, on the other hand, seems to be a listener, a learner. While Martha was running around getting dinner on the table, Mary found great comfort welcoming Jesus into their home and sitting at His feet. Her priority became Jesus.

When Lazarus was sick, it was Martha who rose up quickly to call for Jesus. She was a leader, and she was not going to sit back and take no action. Mary, a follower, stayed and sat still in the house, no doubt, praying and mourning the loss of her brother.

Martha would probably argue that on the day of Jesus' arrival she was focused on Him, but we find her personality got in the way of what should have been her priority. Jesus said, "Mary hath chosen that good part, which shall not be taken away from her." Luke 10:42

There is nothing wrong with being pragmatic or a listener, a leader or a follower. It is what we do with those traits that can lead us to destruction. We cannot allow our personalities on earth to become flesh-filled. When they do, the flesh wins; the glory is lost; and we miss the beautiful, personal design God created us to be.

Study Questions

1. Are you more like Mary or Martha?

2. What one quality do you admire about Martha?

3. What one quality do you admire about Mary?

4. Why do you think God gave you your specific personality?

5. How can you best use your personality traits for the Lord?

Daily Study - Day 3
John 11:2-29; John 12:1-3

Use your strengths. Being made in the image of God is a great privilege and responsibility. We are image bearers, and He has gifted us in ways that should reflect Him. We are quick to list our weaknesses, yet we often have a hard time naming our strengths. We must recognize and lean into the fact that our strength is made perfect in Christ.

This is where Mary and Martha found themselves. They knew their strengths, and they were confident in who God had created them to be.
Martha, that faithful leader, was hospitable. Her home was open to Jesus and probably many others. She was a wonderful hostess and did not mind delegating to accomplish the job at hand. When she recognized a problem, she addressed it. Procrastination seems to be nowhere in her DNA.

Her hospitality allowed her to be in the presence of Jesus and other faithful Christians. Her willingness to get a job done while encouraging others to participate allowed her to accomplish even more. Her haste in running to the Savior to save her brother's life meant only that she loved deeply. Her faith was proven when she proclaimed that He was "the Christ, the Son of God." John 11:27

Mary, the loyal follower, loved to learn. Sitting at Jesus' feet was her greatest desire. She knew how to prioritize the meaningful over the immediate. She proved to be selfless and worshipful through the act of anointing Jesus' feet with her costly ointment. She stayed still and likely pondered the death of her brother.

Her learning allowed her moments with her Savior that no earthly meal could replace. Her priority of walking with Jesus led her to deep moments of worship that even the disciples could not comprehend. Her giving nature assured her that there was no earthly possession that did not first belong to God. Her awe of who He was made the beauty of her soul shine forth for generations.

You see, these strengths of Mary and Martha are different, yet the Lord has used them greatly to accomplish His will. You and I are very different. Our strengths look differently, but there is great purpose within the variety. God wants to pour out His blessings on these strengths so that the world around us can clearly see

Him. Do not shy away. Embrace each one, and ask the Lord to make them perfect through the power of the Holy Spirit.

Study Questions

1. What is one of Martha's strengths that you possess?

2. What is one of Mary's strengths that you possess?

3. How can you use your strengths to help others?

4. What is an example of a time when God used your strengths for His glory?

5. What is a verse that encourages you about God's strength?

Daily Study - Day 4
Read Luke 10:40-41; John 11:6, 20-24

Your weakness is showing. No one wants to appear weak. Martha certainly did not. The task grew, and she was going to handle it. Lazarus died, and she was going to fix it. Ever been there? I certainly have. Life seems to throw curve balls our way daily, and yet, somehow, we are shocked that life's trials have once again come our way.

I am thankful for the example of Martha's weakness in these moments. Otherwise, I would feel as if she was nothing like me. Seeing her human frailty and how Jesus responded gives us a powerful truth that cannot be ignored.

That truth is that we all are weak. I am weak. Say that sentence out loud again. It is hard to say, isn't it? Yet, when we admit that we are weak, it is then that we become strong (2 Corinthians 12:9). God gave us our relationships, our personalities, our strengths, and He also gave us our weaknesses. His desire is not for us to remain weak, but that in our weakness, we find Him.

Do you ever wonder why God allowed Lazarus to die? Why Jesus when he heard that Lazarus was ill waited two days before he even left his location? Sounds pretty cold on the outside looking in, but God had a plan. Go to John 11:27. Martha confesses that she believes that Jesus is the Christ, the Son of God. He wanted to confirm Martha's faith. He wanted her to see that He was the Way, the Truth, and the Life, and that He enabled her to be a living example of her faith in spite of all her weaknesses.

God can use our weaknesses for His glory when we allow them to be seen by others. This does not mean that we flaunt or are proud of our weaknesses. They should be areas that we pray earnestly about and ask the Lord to transform us to be like Him. While being transparent and willing to be less than perfect to others, our lives become a testimony of how God is working.

Stop looking at your weaknesses as your failures. View them as a launching point of greater things to come. Messy weaknesses become ordered examples of God's almighty strength.

Study Questions

1. Is it easier for you to admit your weaknesses or your strengths?

2. What weakness would you like to change if you could?

3. How can God turn your weakness into strength?

4. Who was the last person you shared your weakness with?

5. Write down a verse that claims the victory over weakness and pray about it this week.

Daily Study - Day 5
Read John 12:1-9

Our response affects our outcome. I love a good ending to a story. We have journeyed through Mary and Martha's relationship, their personality, their strengths and their weaknesses. Did they learn from these events that took place in their lives? Lessons can be taught, but until the lessons are applied, they are just simply information.

John 12 gives us insight into how the Lord used these lessons both in Mary and Martha's lives. We find here another gathering, a meal, and guess who serves that meal? You're right! It is Martha. She did not stop doing what she loved. She just did it with the right spirit. There is no grumbling or hasty spirit found in these verses.

Mary finds herself moving beyond learning at Jesus's side to worshiping at His feet. She learned from the Master and now, she is willing to get on her knees, pour out her most expensive ointment, and carefully wash her Savior's feet with her hair. Nothing else matters but her devotion to Him.

Remember the dead brother? We cannot overlook the fact that Lazarus is present sitting at this table. The brother that Mary and Martha took care of and prayed for. He was a living miracle that strengthened their faith!

Having an extra mouth to feed, watching her sister pour out a very costly possession, and knowing the ridicule that was coming from within the room and without the city, did not waiver Martha's spirit. She was strong in her faith and in her leadership. She was steady in her abilities. She was honest with her weaknesses. She was dependent on her Savior.

I wonder what it is that we need to respond to correctly? God is always working in us. He is always drawing us. He is forever changing us. The outcome lies in our decision to follow His supernatural working power. May we respond like Mary and Martha. We cannot blame God for busy, uncomfortable, and many times, challenging situations. We must lean into them and ask the Lord to shape our will into His, and to make His priorities our priorities. It is there that we will find perfect peace and joy and change in His ever-loving presence.

Study Questions

1. In what ways has God been speaking to you through your present circumstances?

2. How often do you look at God's corrections as a blessing?

3. Name one area of spiritual growth that you have seen in your life this past year?

4. What life outcome are you longing for?

5. How can your life be an example of growth in Christ to others?

The Proverbs 31 Mother
Three Warnings from Proverbs

ENCOURAGEMENT FROM WOMEN

Week 3 - Video Session Notes
The Proverbs 31 Mother: Three Warnings from Proverbs

Introduction:

_____

_____

_____

_____

I. A Warning About _____.

What, my son? and what, the son of my womb? and what, the son of my vows? Give not thy strength unto women, nor thy ways to that which destroyeth kings. Proverbs 31:2-3

II. A Warning About _____.

It is not for kings, O Lemuel, it is not for kings to drink wine; nor for princes strong drink: Lest they drink, and forget the law, and pervert the judgment of any of the afflicted. Give strong drink unto him that is ready to perish, and wine unto those that be of heavy hearts. Let him drink, and forget his poverty, and remember his misery no more. Proverbs 31:4-7

III. A Warning About _____.

Open thy mouth for the dumb in the cause of all such as are appointed to destruction. Open thy mouth, judge righteously, and plead the cause of the poor and needy. Proverbs 31:8-9

Conclusion:

_____

_____

_____

_____

Answers: *women, wine, words*

Daily Study - Day 1
Read Proverbs 31:1-9

Use your influence for God and for good. This is the message the mother of the king in Proverbs 31 was teaching. As we look at the book of Proverbs, we know Solomon wrote much of this book filled with great wisdom, but as we get to chapter 31 we find a king named Lemuel as the author. If we look back in the Old Testament through the generations of the kings, we cannot find a king with this name. If we look a little closer, we learn the name Lemuel means, "for God" or "belonging to God." Some scholars believe this was actually King Solomon writing and giving himself this name as one who was created "for God" Himself. Another possibility is that Lemuel was a nickname given to him by his mother Bathsheba. While we cannot know for sure, it does bring an interesting thought to consider this could be Solomon speaking about what his mother, Bathsheba taught him. You might remember Bathsheba as the beautiful woman who David saw bathing herself.

Solomon was not only wealthy and wise, he also had some big battles he faced and this chapter of Proverbs gives us a prophetic glimpse of what those battles possibly looked like. If we look back in 1 Kings 11:3, we find this fact about Solomon, "And he had seven hundred wives, princesses, and three hundred concubines: and his wives turned away his heart." Whether this proverb is from Solomon's recollections or not, we can take the truths found within this proverb and glean some big lessons.

In this narrative that is written just as a mother might speak in a moment of firm teaching, we find the warnings of the mother laid out plainly for the son who had wealth and influence.

A king's life would not only be marked by great influence, but also by great impact. How he lived, the woman, or in his case the hundreds of *women* he chose, and the way he pursued his moral choices would strongly determine how he used his resources and words. His mother is simply saying, "use your influence for God, and for good." If he didn't, she knew the outcome would lead to great distress for both the king and for those over whom he ruled.

Her warnings included being aware of women, wine, and words. While we women don't necessarily receive the warnings the same a son would, what we can gather is this - we have a great responsibility to use our influence for God and for good. Whether we are influencing children in a classroom, at church, home, or in the community - the message is the same - use your influence for God and for good.

Study Questions

1. Who in your life has influenced you toward the wisdom of God and His Word?

2. Who in your life are you influencing currently? (think of those you come in contact with regularly)

3. What is one way you can take your influence to the next level with one of those you are impacting in your life?

Daily Study – Day 2
Read Proverbs 31:1-2, John 1:12-13

Three questions. The mother asks her son three rhetorical questions in this soliloquy. They are found in Proverbs 31:2.

1. What my son?
2. What the son of my womb?
3. What the son of my vows?

The mother is pointing out a few reminders right away.

First, she reminds her son who he is. I imagine if we could dig a little deeper into her heart, we might hear her say, "You are my son. And my son has been taught to discern between right and wrong."

Second, you are my blood. I can almost hear her saying, "I gave birth to you. You have a responsibility to our family to do right."

Thirdly, you are the son of my vows to our Almighty God. You are a treasured son that I have brought to the Lord and promised to Him.

Her entire tone is implying, "How dare you make a decision that would disgrace yourself and your mother." Three times she addresses him as if to say, LISTEN UP! I have some valuable truth to share with you, my son. LISTEN. TO. ME.

The truth we find in her bold declaration to her son is a truth we can apply to our lives as we remember who we are in Christ. Each of the questions she brought to him addressed his identity. Who He was, was foundational for how he behaved. The mother wanted her son to revisit who He was and where He came from. He was hers. He was her bloodline. He was her answer to prayer from God.

Our identity in Christ gives us a foundation on which to build our behavior. When we remember that we are God's daughters, that we are under the blood of Jesus, and that we are uniquely designed by a magnificent Creator, we will live differently. While we cannot know for sure every thought in this mother's heart, we can glean from her wisdom. One nugget of truth to hold to is the power of your identity for in that identification as a child of God, you have a great responsibility to walk and live as a follower of Jesus Christ.

Study Questions

1. Fill in the blanks to describe your identity as a follower of Jesus. I am God's_____. I am covered by the blood of _____. I am forgiven for all my _____.

2. Why is identity important?

3. Give one reason why you think the mother wanted her son to remember his identity.

4. How do we keep from taking on a false identity in the confusing world we live in?

Daily Study - Day 3
Read Proverbs 31:3 and 31:10-19

Three warnings. There are not only three questions that the mother asked her son like we learned yesterday, but there are three warnings the mother gives her son before she gets into teaching him what a virtuous woman truly is. For the next three days, we are going to unpack each warning.

The first one is found in Proverbs 31:3, "Give not thy strength unto women, nor thy ways to that which destroyeth kings."

The mother is teaching her son that there are two paths in life. One leads to victory. The other leads to destruction. While it might be easy for a mature believer to clearly see the difference between these two paths, the enemy is very good at making the path seem cloudy or justifying why one path might seem okay to explore. I think it's safe to say, this son had explored the path of ungodly women. This is why we have this passage of Scripture from a mother to a son. The mother is very passionate about correcting her son's wrong behavior of allowing women to have his time and attention.

The warning of not giving his strength to women comes as a caution to not give his heart away to a woman who would lead his heart away from God. Bathsheba was in no way telling him that he should steer clear of all women, but rather that he should avoid any woman who does not have a heart for the Lord. As we find later in the chapter, his mother outlines specific characteristics of a woman who would be worthy of his time and attention – one who would make a virtuous wife. Such a woman would keep his heart safe, work hard, honor God, and care for her family.

Study Questions

1. Why do you think the mother specifically warned her son about ungodly women?

2. Have you ever had an ungodly friend influence you?

3. Why is it important to guard your heart?

4. What is one thing we can learn from the description of the woman described in Proverbs 31:10-19?

Daily Study - Day 4
Read Proverbs 31:4-5 and Proverbs 31:15-19

The second warning. The second warning the mother brings up is the warning about drinking alcohol. While there is much to teach here, her main purpose and instruction comes due to his responsibility. Proverbs 31:4-5 says, "It is not for kings, O Lemuel, it is not for kings to drink wine; nor for princes strong drink: Lest they drink, and forget the law, and pervert the judgment of any of the afflicted."

The purpose of avoiding the alcohol was so that the king could rightly fulfill his role of keeping the law and judging rightly. Once alcohol is consumed and hinders the mental capacity, no longer could the king fulfill his role as a trusted leader.

We can glean two things from this lesson the mother was teaching.

First, alcohol inhibits influence. Basically being under the influence forfeits your influence. This alone is one of the reasons we know alcohol is not a good idea.

Secondly, we as daughters of the king have a royal responsibility to fulfill the God-given role in each of our lives to lead those in our sphere of influence. It could be in the home, in the workplace, in our ministry, or in other areas of life where God prompts your heart to lead an individual or a group. But you cannot lead well, if you are leaning on a substance other than the Word of God. Let God's Word be the thing that influences your mind to influence others.

Later in the chapter we find the mother describing the woman worthy of the king's time and attention as one who gets up early, and has good reasoning skills, and leads a disciplined life. It's not one who gives into her fleshly desires or who goes with the flow of culture. She sets the tone for right and abides with the Lord so that she can fulfill her God-given assignments.

Study Questions

1. Have you seen how alcohol affects a person in a negative way?

2. Why is influencing others important?

3. Who in your life do you want to influence the most? And why?

4. Is there anything in your life you need to change in order to be a better influence?

Daily Study - Day 5
Read Proverbs 31:8-9 and Proverbs 31:20-31

The final warning. The final warning from the mother to the son comes in the form of an instruction to open his mouth wisely for those who cannot speak for themselves. Proverbs 31:8-9. "Open thy mouth for the dumb in the cause of all such as are appointed to destruction. Open thy mouth, judge righteously, and plead the cause of the poor and needy."

There are a couple groups of people mentioned here that we can take note of. The first is "the dumb." These are those who cannot speak for themselves. The others are the poor and those in need.

The mother's heart for her son was for him to see those who were less important in men's eyes. She wanted her son to not only take note of the unfortunate, but to act on their behalf by speaking up for them.

Once again we find the mother of the king reminding him of his responsibility to use his influence for good. While he could have anyone he wanted by his side or in his courtyard, the mother reminded him to use his voice to lift the broken, help the hurting, and feed the hungry.

The lesson for us is simple. Use words wisely to defend the ones who cannot defend themselves. Practically it might look like standing up for a friend, speaking up when someone is gossipped about, giving to those who don't have, loving a child in foster care, mentoring a teenager who doesn't have a godly mother, or just saying something when no one else will speak the truth.

The virtuous woman passage of Scripture comes from a mother who is weary and heavy-hearted for a son who seems to possibly have rebelled. Rather than a laundry list of things for us to live up to, it's a lesson of instruction for us to pass on to the next generation to remember who they are in Christ so that they can use their influence for God and for good.

Study Questions

1. Has anyone ever used their words to hurt you?

2. How did that affect you?

3. Why are words so important?

4. Who is someone in your life who needs to hear words of hope and truth from you?

5. Name one person you can send a "thank you" text or card to for speaking helpful words for you or to you. Send the text or note today.

Encountering Christ
What Happens When Women Meet With Jesus

Week 4 - Video Session Notes
Encountering Christ:
What Happens When Women Meet With Jesus

Introduction:

_____

_____

_____

_____

I. To those waiting for redemption, _____ for He is here.

Luke 2:38
And she coming in that instant gave thanks likewise unto the Lord, and spake of him to all them that looked for redemption in Jerusalem.

II. To those in need of healing, He has a _____ waiting for you.

Mark 5:34
And he said unto her, Daughter, thy faith hath made thee whole; go in peace, and be whole of thy plague.

III. To those who are worn and weary, He provides _____.

Luke 8:2-3
And certain women, which had been healed of evil spirits and infirmities, Mary called Magdalene, out of whom went seven devils, and Joanna the wife of Chuza Herod's steward, and Susanna, and many others, which ministered unto him of their substance.

IV. To those overcome by guilt and shame, He has _____ you.

Luke 7:47
My head with oil thou didst not anoint: but this woman hath anointed my feet with ointment. Wherefore I say unto thee, Her sins, which are many, are forgiven; for she loved much: but to whom little is forgiven, the same loveth little.

V. To those desperately trying to escape the chaos and confusion, He gives _____.

Matthew 15:22, 25, 28
And, behold, a woman of Canaan came out of the same coasts, and cried unto him, saying, Have mercy on me, O Lord, thou son of David; my daughter is grievously vexed with a devil. Then came she and worshipped him, saying, Lord, help me. Then Jesus answered and said unto her, O woman, great is thy faith: be it unto thee even as thou wilt. And her daughter was made whole from that very hour.

Conclusion:

_____
_____
_____
_____

If to Jesus we would draw near, we would be able to live in faith, not fear.

Answers: *Praise, Promise, Renewed Passion, Pardoned, Peace*

Daily Study – Day 1
Read Luke 2:36-38

An encounter with Jesus brings praise. In these few short verses we are introduced to Anna, the prophetess. Luke interrupts the narrative of Jesus' birth and earthly beginnings to introduce us to an otherwise insignificant woman. As an elderly widow, this woman would have meant virtually nothing in Jewish society. However, in keeping with the theme of Luke, there is an emphasis here on how the gospel became accessible to ALL through Jesus. Because of Jesus, all who come and call on His name for salvation would be welcomed, loved, accepted, and kept by Him.

We know she was a daughter of Phanuel, of the Israelite tribe of Asher, an elderly widow; however, we see that before her heritage, she was also titled a prophetess. Anna, whose name means favor or grace, was one of five prophetesses in Scripture. I find it interesting that she was identified spiritually before she was identified physically.

Though unexpected, it was no accident that Anna had an encounter with the infant Jesus while she was praying at the Temple. She was a Jew and would have been well aware of the promise of a coming Messiah. We don't know that she was looking specifically for the arrival of Jesus, but she was faithfully doing what she always did, praying and fasting. God surely meets us where we are, and we can be sure He directs where we must go, as well as who we must be after that special meeting. There is truly the glorious in the mundane, and in the middle of our service we see those truly amazing displays of the goodness of God in the land of the living. Anna's humility gave her the freedom to fully live out her faith.

The Bible says, when she encountered the infant Christ, she "gave thanks."Here the Greek word is *anthomologeomai* which means, "to acknowledge fully, to celebrate fully in praise with thanksgiving." Likewise, praise should be our response when we are in the presence of God. Her actions show us that she personally believed the promise of God to send His Son, and when she received the promise of God there was nothing that kept her from making that belief public. Anna is even hailed by some as the first Christian missionary because of her response to an encounter with the infant Jesus.

There are no words that could sum up the experience of being in the presence of God and seeing the fulfillment of His promise; therefore, praise is the only proper response. Praise and proclamation were Anna's response to her encounter with the infant Jesus and encouragement of redemption to come. May those who listen to us hear us speak of Him, what He's done, what He's doing, and what He will do.

Study Questions

1. What did you learn about Jesus through the account of Anna the Prophetess?

2. Who were the other four prophetesses in Scripture? See Numbers 12, Judges 4-5, Hebrews 11:32-34, II Kings 22: 14-20, II Chronicles 34:22-33, Isaiah 8:3

3. How have you incorporated praise and thanksgiving into your everyday life?

4. Has your praise been followed by proclamation and sharing the Gospel? When was the last time you shared the Gospel with someone?

5. Read I John 1:9, Acts 2:21, Romans 10:9-10, John 11:25…. Reflect- Have you put any caveats or limitations on the Gospel?

Daily Study – Day 2
Read Matthew 9:20-22, Mark 5:25-34, Luke 8:43-48

An encounter with Jesus brings a promise. This unnamed woman was known by her issue, and while an unfortunate identity, it was only logical. She spent at least 12 years of her life being controlled by her disease. Her issue, which the Gospel writers tell us was one involving blood, would have meant weakness, isolation, and embarrassment. This woman, though known by her fragile body, would eventually meet Jesus, and she would be forever known by her faith.

Levitical law deemed this woman ritually unclean. She was unfit to worship or take part in Temple services. Leviticus 15 goes into detail concerning the laws surrounding those with "an issue of blood" and the cleansing that would need to happen should she touch or be touched. Not only did her infirmity plague her, but also everyone she came in contact with. It is likely that this made her life lonely and lifeless.While her issue did not make her impure, in the sense of wrongdoing, she was, by Jewish standards, ceremonially unclean.

With this knowledge, it makes sense that she spent all her living to gain relief of her ailment (Luke 8:43). The Bible says that this woman found nothing and no one that could provide her with the relief she desired. Her own attempts to better herself and fix her situation came up short, just as our desire to make ourselves worthy will always end in failure. For all her striving, she only grew worse. For 12 years she suffered at the hands of physicians who were unable to help her. The moment she encountered Christ and touched His hem, however, she was cleansed and made whole. I love what Herbert Lockyer said about the woman and her issue, "Where men failed, Christ succeeded."

Jesus commended this woman by telling her "thy faith hath made thee whole." While it was Jesus who surely made her whole, it wasn't the touch but her tender faith that resulted in the touch. She believed the person, promise, and power of God to bring healing. Here the Greek word for faith , *pistis ,* is a noun meaning "reliance upon God for salvation". Her faith replaced her fear when she encountered Jesus for she knew He would be her salvation. If we draw near, we have available to us all the promises of God. Hebrews 11:6 says, "But without faith it is impossible to please him: for he that cometh to God must believe that he is, and that he is a rewarder of them that diligently seek him." Come to Him, claim the promise, and go in peace.

Study Questions

1. What did you learn about Jesus through the account of this woman?

2. What are some of the things we turn to for salvation other than God?

3. What promise of God is especially dear to you?

4. We find the definition of faith in Hebrews 11:1. Write the definition of faith in your own words.

Daily Study - Day 3
Read Matthew 27: 56, 61; 28:1; Mark 15:40, 47; 16: 1-19; Luke 8:2, 24:10, and John 19:25, and 20:1-18

An encounter with Jesus brings passion. We are introduced to Mary Magdalene in the Gospel of Matthew, and we continue to see her in the other 3 Gospels. Each of the Gospels speak to us of Jesus' ministry in detail, and upon reading, Mary is found to be one of the main contributors to His ministry (Luke 8:3; Mark 15:41). It is interesting to note that in each account of Mary Magdalene, Jesus was always near. Mary is mentioned 14 times throughout the Gospels. We see through her life and the lives of others that Jesus had come to seek and to save all who were lost (Luke 19:10).

The town of Magdala was a thriving port city of Galilee, and it was the known home of Mary. We have no record of her family or relations; however, we do know that Mary was associated with affliction, but was later overcome with affection.

Mary Magdalene has often been put on a pedestal as a graciously forgiven fornicator and fallen woman. Many look at the account in Luke 7, and they claim Mary Magdalene to be the unnamed woman; however, there is little evidence and much debate as to whether Mary Magdalene had such a sordid and promiscuous past. There are countless ministries that bear her namesake as a reminder that Jesus redeems ALL who come to Him. Scripture does tell us that Mary was possessed with devils from which Jesus released her, and redemption was very much a part of her story (Luke 8:2). Either way, she was a sinner, Jesus became her Savior, and the grace of God had no less effect on her sinful state.

The focus has often been on her mess; however, after her encounter with Jesus, Mary Magdalene began a life of ministry. She and other women who followed Jesus, "ministered unto him out of their substance." The word "minister" in the Greek is *diakoneō,* which means to minister or attend to the needs of others. The Greek word for substance is *huparchonta,* which means, "a sense of goods, property, wealth, goods, and possessions". Mary must have had some sort of income or means, and upon her encounter with Jesus, she supported Him and helped to facilitate His earthly ministry.

No doubt, Mary was compelled to serve Jesus out of a deep sense of love, gratitude, and belief. She had an encounter with Christ in which she experienced His power, and it gave her a passion for service. For it is impossible to be in the presence of God and walk away unchanged.

Study Questions

1. What did you learn about Jesus through the life and story of Mary Magdalene?

2. Why is passionate service so important in the life of the believer? How are the two concepts (passion and service) related?

3. Mary used her substance to minister/serve. Name some of the ways in which you can specifically minister as unto the Lord?

4. What does Galatians 5:13-14 say about passion and stewarding our freedom in Christ?

5. Mary had her last encounter with Christ recorded in all four Gospels. What role do you think her passion played in this crucial encounter?

Daily Study - Day 4
Read Luke 7:36-50

An encounter with Jesus brings pardon. It is no wonder that we find ourselves back in the book of Luke. As mentioned earlier this week, this book of the Bible highlights the availability of the Gospel to all. At the beginning of this scene, we find Jesus at the home of Simon, the Pharisee. Jesus had been invited, but there is indication that He was not truly welcome (Luke 7:44-46). From what we know of cultural expectations, this would prove to be a lack of hospitality shown by Simon. Additionally, if there were no intentions of slight it showed the lack of significance that Simon had for Jesus.

However, the focus of this passage is not Simon and his slight, but this woman and her Savior. It is clear from the onset that this woman did not just sin, but openly and publicly committed sinful acts. The suggestion here is something promiscuous; however, the text does not clearly state her sin. The omission of these details mirrors the truth written in the Valley of Vision, "Let me never forget that the heinousness of sin lies not so much in the nature of the sin committed, as in the greatness of the Person sinned against." Psalm 51:4, reminds us that all sin is against God and that is the most grievous.

There were no words recorded from the woman, no apologies made, no pleas, no explanations, just undeniable penitent action is recorded for us to read. With her affection for the Master on display, we know she knew there was a cost of discipleship. The ointment was costly, her pride was costly, but the price of her sin was far greater. What she did was an act of worship, but it was with her faith, not her worship, that Jesus concerned Himself.

Jesus did not shy away from calling out sin in her, but He did not condemn her (Luke 7: 47). There is a difference between correction and condemnation, the former focuses on the Savior and the latter focuses on the sin. Salvation from sin only comes through the Savior. When we are pardoned, forgiven by God, will not be sinless, but we should sin less. "Thy sins are forgiven…Thy faith hath saved thee: go in peace." (Luke 7: 48 & 50) No doubt she wondered what Jesus' response to her would be. However, in keeping with His character, He loved, forgave, and saved.

Study Questions

1. What did you learn about Jesus through His encounter with this woman?

2. The Pharisees had much to say about this woman and her public display of penance. Read Luke 15:11-32. What would be the right and Christian response to a repentant sinner?

3. Read Romans 3-4. What does it mean to be "forgiven" by Jesus?

4. Read and paraphrase John 3:15-18

Daily Study - Day 5
Read Matthew 15:21-28 and Mark 7:24-30

An encounter with Jesus brings peace. This woman is found in the Gospels of Matthew and Mark. She is often identified by her home of Sidon and called the Syrophoenician woman. First, we see her desperation upon coming into contact with Jesus. She was worried for her daughter who was possessed by demons. Many a mother has grieved over the spiritual strongholds present in her childrens' lives. Matthew Henry said, "The vexations of children are the trouble of parents, and nothing should be more so than their being under the power of Satan". While in her desperation she met Jesus, and her worry became the vehicle for peace that only Jesus could bring. She came to him needing one thing, but she left with everything.

Matthew and Mark have identified this woman by her location, and some scholars believe this highlights the elitism present in that day. In Matthew, she is known as the "woman of Canaan", and in Mark, she is called a "Greek." Both titles allude to the fact that she was a Gentile. Her desperation must have kept her pride and any personal animosity at bay. For as we read the Scripture, we see she humbled herself, both in word and deed. This woman understood her position, and she understood Jesus was the promise (Matthew 15:22). As the Son of David, a Messianic title, she knew that He was a part of the covenant promise available to the children of Israel, and she, a daughter of Canaan, was a stranger to that promise.

Matthew says that she cried out to Him for mercy on behalf of her daughter, yet her impassioned plea was met with silence and dismissal from Jesus. Jesus does eventually answer her, but His whole response seems out of character. Was he merely questioning or testing her faith? There is much debate on what Jesus responded and why He responded to this woman the way that He did. What is clear is that He was not required to help her. Nevertheless, she persisted in her plea, Jesus honored and encouraged her faith, and she gained peace for her daughter.

I once heard someone make the statement that, "Jesus promises a peace that passeth all understanding, not peace because of understanding." Her encounter with Jesus, though unique, impacted her life and the life of her family. We don't know the expectations of her encounter, but we have an idea of what she experienced. Relief, joy, and gratitude fill the heart of a parent whose child has been made whole. May we recognize and rest in the truth that an encounter with Jesus leads to peace with God and the peace of God. We see again that it is impossible to be in the presence of God and walk away unchanged.

Study Questions

1. Read both Gospel accounts and compare/contrast. How do the accounts fall in line with the themes and purposes of each book?

2. What did you learn about Jesus through His encounter with this woman?

3. What is to be done when it seems silence is Christ's response to the cries of our hearts?

4. How has meeting Christ impacted your life and the lives of others?

The Samaritan Woman
Recognizing Divine Appointments

Week 5 - Video Session Notes
The Samaritan Woman:
Recognizing Divine Appointments

Introduction:

_____

_____

_____

_____

I.   The _____ Served As A Reminder Of The Past.

And he must needs go through Samaria. Then cometh he to a city of Samaria, which is called Sychar, near to the parcel of ground that Jacob gave to his son Joseph. Now Jacob's well was there. Jesus therefore, being wearied with his journey, sat thus on the well: and it was about the sixth hour. John 4:4-6

II.   The _____ Showed Her What She Was Truly Lacking.

There cometh a woman of Samaria to draw water: Jesus saith unto her, Give me to drink. (For his disciples were gone away unto the city to buy meat.) Then saith the woman of Samaria unto him, How is it that thou, being a Jew, askest drink of me, which am a woman of Samaria? for the Jews have no dealings with the Samaritans. Jesus answered and said unto her, If thou knewest the gift of God, and who it is that saith to thee, Give me to drink; thou wouldest have asked of him, and he would have given thee living water. The woman saith unto him, Sir, thou hast nothing to draw with, and the well is deep: from whence then hast thou that living water? Art thou greater than our father Jacob, which gave us the well, and drank thereof himself, and his children, and his cattle? Jesus answered and said unto her, Whosoever drinketh of this water shall thirst again: But whosoever drinketh of the water that I shall give him shall never thirst; but the water that I shall give him shall be in him a well of water springing up into everlasting life. The woman saith unto him, Sir, give me this water, that I thirst not, neither come hither to draw. John 4:7-15

III.   The _____ Revealed A Misplaced Devotion.

The woman saith unto him, Sir, I perceive that thou art a prophet. Our fathers worshipped in this mountain; and ye say, that in Jerusalem is the place where men ought to worship. Jesus saith unto her, Woman, believe me, the hour cometh, when ye shall neither in this mountain, nor yet at Jerusalem, worship the Father. Ye worship ye know not what: we know what we worship: for salvation is of the Jews. But the hour cometh, and now is, when the true worshippers shall worship the Father in spirit and in truth: for the Father seeketh such to worship him. God is a Spirit: and they that worship him must worship him in spirit and in truth. The woman saith unto him, I know that Messias cometh, which is called Christ: when he is come, he will tell us all things. Jesus saith unto her, I that speak unto thee am he. The woman then left her waterpot, and went her way into the city... John 4:19-26, 28

IV.   The _____ Needs To Be Done.

And upon this came his disciples, and marvelled that he talked with the woman: yet no man said, What seekest thou? or, Why talkest thou with her? In the mean while his disciples prayed him, saying, Master, eat. But he said unto them, I have meat to eat that ye know not of. Therefore said the disciples one to another, Hath any man brought him ought to eat? Jesus saith unto them, My meat is to do the will of him that sent me, and to finish his work. Say not ye, There are yet four months, and then cometh harvest? behold, I say unto you, Lift up your eyes, and look on the fields; for they are white already to harvest. And he that reapeth receiveth wages, and gathereth fruit unto life eternal: that both he that soweth and he that reapeth may rejoice together. And herein is that saying true, One soweth, and another reapeth. I sent you to reap that whereon ye bestowed no labour: other men laboured, and ye are entered into their labours. John 4:27, 31-38

V.   The _____ That Matters Most.

The woman then left her waterpot, and went her way into the city, and saith to the men, Come, see a man, which told me all things that ever I did: is not this the Christ? Then they went out of the city, and came unto him. And many of the Samaritans of that city believed on him for the saying of the woman, which testified, He told me all that ever I did. So when the Samaritans were come unto him, they besought him that he would tarry with them: and he abode there two days. And many more believed because of his own word; And said unto the woman, Now we believe, not because of thy saying: for we have heard him ourselves, and know that this is indeed the Christ, the Saviour of the world. Now after two days he departed thence, and went into Galilee. John 4:28-30, 39-43

Conclusion:

_____
_____
_____
_____

Answers: *Well, Water, Worship, Work, Word*

Daily Study - Day 1
Read John 4:4-6

Brokenness is found in every person's story; past, present, and future. No one is exempt from hurt and heartache, sorrow and suffering, or distress and despair. This is precisely where we find the Samaritan woman at the well. We don't even know her name, but we can see glimpses of her pain.

The Samaritans lived in Samaria, which is north of Jerusalem. They were a biracial people. This came about when the Israelites of the Northern Kingdom were taken captive by Assyria in the Old Testament times. Some Israelites chose to remain in Assyria when they were allowed to return home. This led to intermarriages between the Israelites and the Assyrians. Bringing us the Samaritan people. So, they had both Jewish and Gentile (a Gentile is anyone not of Jewish nationality) roots.

Because of this, the Jewish people hated the Samaritans and had no dealings with them. They were considered "less than." Racism goes far beyond our here and now.

Jacobs Well is where we find Jesus stopping to rest on His journey. The well was a special place. It was where Jacob, who had been estranged from his brother, bought for one hundred pieces of money (Genesis 33:18-19). This is where he returned home physically, emotionally, and spiritually. Jacob had run away. He had married, and the family didn't worship the God of Israel, Jehovah. This land was so much more than just land. It was homecoming. When he set up camp, he built an altar and called it El-elohe-Israel, meaning the Mighty One – God of Israel (Genesis 33:20). It is fitting that Jesus would stop here to rest along His way.

The well met the physical needs of those who lived nearby. It gave fresh water for people to drink. It was also used as a place for socializing. The women, in particular, would gather for community connections. The well was the social network of its day.

This is where we jump into the Samaritan Woman's story. She is coming upon the well where Jesus is resting. It is the sixth hour of the day, noon. When she arrives at the well, Jesus immediately asks her for a drink of water. In the

Jewish culture, she wasn't even worthy of communicating with, but Jesus didn't care about the opinions of others. He goes against the norm of society and speaks to this broken woman.

We know she is broken because of the time of day she was coming to the well. It was in the heat of the day. The ladies of her culture went in the early morning or late evening because of the scorching heat. But here she is. Alone. She wasn't worthy by her own people's standards because of her life choices. The well served as a reminder of her past.

She was a woman of compromised integrity. She was looking to fill a longing, a void, and she was searching for it in men. Jesus didn't mind her reputation. He wanted to give her an opportunity for a changed life.

He wants to do the same for you.

Jesus is in the business of rescuing, restoring, and renewing. He doesn't look at your past or present to decide whether you are worthy or not of His forgiveness, mercy, and grace. He looks at you and sees what He can make you be…. a NEW CREATION IN CHRIST.

2 Corinthians 5:17
"Therefore if any man be in Christ, he is a new creature: old things are passed away; behold, all things are become new."

Find hope in that. You, or anyone else, are never too far gone for Jesus to save.

Study Questions

1. The name El-elohe-Israel means the Mighty One. Explain how this name and character trait of God has been made personal in your life through a specific trial.

2. We read how racism, social injustices, and elitism is nothing new. The Bible reminds us in Ecclesiastes 1:9 that *"...there is no new thing under the sun."* Have you ever been made to feel less than by another person's standard? Have you ever been the one to make someone else feel inferior? Tell of a time in your life when you have seen this played out (directly or indirectly) and how you responded (directly or indirectly).

3. We live in a broken world. Sometimes we suffer hurt inflicted upon us by others, and sometimes we reap the consequences of our sin. You might feel as though you are too far for redemption. You are not alone in your brokenness. You are not isolated in your pain. Others have been there. Do you have a past that haunts you? Jesus understands and wants to meet you in your pain. He wants to heal you and set you free. Read Luke 4:16-21. Write verses 18 and 19 and ponder on the action words. Then find HOPE in verse 21, where Jesus says, *"This day is the scripture fulfilled in your ears."* Jesus is the fulfillment of the Scripture. He is the ANSWER to your brokenness.

Daily Study - Day 2
Read John 4:7-15

Water is vital for survival. We need a lot of water for our bodies to function correctly. Without the correct amount of water, our bodies will suffer dehydration. Dehydration has many side effects, like kidney stones, unclear thinking, mood swings, and much more. Science tells us that a person would die within a few days without water. Water is important.

The Samaritan Woman comes to the well to get water when she thinks no one will be there. She was an outcast of her people. She had made some horrible decisions involving men and marriage, and because of these choices, she has been marked by shame and ridicule. She seemingly has no friends and goes to the well at the hottest point of the day with her water pot to fetch water.

Remember, a well is a place of social gathering. Women of the day would go and chat and catch up as they were going about their daily tasks. This woman didn't join them.

She comes upon the well and sees a man. Not just any man, a JEW. Samaritans and Jews were not friends. This Man dares to ask her for a drink of water. Her prejudice towards Him spews out of her mouth.

Prejudice is nothing new. The Bible tells us in Ecclesiastes 1:8-9 that there is nothing new under the sun. Jesus wanted to break down these prejudices. He knew the only way to do that was through Himself. Jesus is the answer to our moral and social injustices.

Next, we see Jesus continuing to speak to this woman in a tender but informative tone. He lets her know that if she knew who He was, she would ask Him for a drink of water. Not just any water, but LIVING WATER.

The Samaritan Woman's response slowly begins shifting. She now goes from calling Jesus a JEW to SIR. However, her attitude remains.

Jesus continues to tell her of this water that satisfies. She desires so much not to have to go to this well. It is a constant reminder of her failures and her shame. Her longing for this Water shows what she is truly lacking.

Jesus is offering this woman Water that would quench her thirst forever. He wanted to give her LIVING WATER. This Water would fill her full of Himself, which is complete satisfaction.

Jesus wants to offer Himself wholly to you, too. He is the only Source of this Water. He is the One and Only Way of salvation.

Jesus went to the cross, sacrificing His life for you and me (and the entire world) so that we might have life and have it more abundantly.

John 10:9-10
"I am the door: by me if any man enter in, he shall be saved, and shall go in and out, and find pasture. The thief cometh not, but for to steal, and to kill, and to destroy: I am come that they might have life, and that they might have it more abundantly."

Jesus hung on the cross for our sins, and He is the only way for our sins to be washed away (Psalm 51, Hebrews 10:22, and Ephesians 5:26).

Jesus is the Water of Life, and He is the Gift offered to all those who thirst.

Revelation 22:16-17
"I Jesus have sent mine angel to testify unto you these things in the churches. I am the root and the offspring of David, and the bright and morning star. And the Spirit and the bride say, Come. And let him that heareth say, Come. And let him that is athirst come. And whosoever will, let him take the water of life freely."

Are you saved and satisfied?

Study Questions

1. Why was the woman surprised at the request of Jesus? This woman was an outcast by her people because of her poor choices in life. Have you ever reached outside of your comfort zone and shown kindness or befriended someone that others might look down on? Ask the Lord to help you to see past the surface of people you meet and see them as Jesus sees them… empty, longing, and needing Jesus.

2. We all have goals and aspirations in life. Does yours revolve around the material, financial, career, social, and relationship gains, or do they revolve around the filling only Jesus can give? This isn't a question regarding salvation but rather a satisfaction of the spirit. Write out Matthew 5:6 *"Blessed are they which do hunger and thirst after righteousness: for they shall be filled."* Don't be full of the things that leave you longing. Are you truly hungry and thirsty for righteousness?

3. What do you have an appetite for? What you desire is what you will devour. Good or bad, you will fill your time, treasure, and talents with it. Desire righteous living. John 6:35 *"And Jesus said unto them, I am the bread of life: he that cometh to me shall never hunger; and he that believeth on me shall never thirst."* Are you hungry and thirsty for Jesus? Write out a prayer to the Lord confessing what you have been hungry for and what you have been full of. Then get freedom and cleansing by the washing of the water and the blood of Jesus. Read and meditate on Hebrews 10:19-25.

Daily Study - Day 3
Read John 4:19-26, 28

"We must never rest until everything inside us worships God." – A.W. Tozer.

Worship is so much more than the song service at church. Worship comes from an old Anglo-Saxon word meaning "worthship." This is a proclamation of worthiness. Who is worthy of our worship?

Psalm 18:1-3
"I will love thee, O Lord, my strength. The Lord is my rock, and my fortress, and my deliverer; my God, my strength, in whom I will trust; my buckler, and the horn of my salvation, and my high tower. I will call upon the Lord, who is worthy to be praised: so shall I be saved from mine enemies."

Only the Lord is worthy of our worship. This is where we pick up the Samaritan Woman's story.

She has been filling the void in her life with misplaced devotion. She has sought acceptance and love from men. She has devoted her energy to things that will ultimately disappoint her. Jesus goes straight for her heart with His pointed command. "Go, call thy husband, and come hither." In those days a woman couldn't enter into an agreement or contract without her husband's approval.

I can only imagine her hanging her head as she responded in the next verse. *"I have no husband."* Another reminder of her stained past. Another dig at her failures in life. She must feel like she can't escape who she is. She is defeated.

Jesus responds to her honest and pitiful comment with mercy and truth. He doesn't condemn. He calls out the truth. She has had five husbands, and the man she is with now isn't her husband. Jesus has a way of exposing our innermost secrets with His Light.

Now she changes what she calls Him once again. She calls Him a PROPHET. She is taken aback by the fact that He knows the truth about her and continues to communicate with her.

The physical layers are starting to be peeled back to reveal the spiritual. She makes a statement regarding the differences in worship between the Samaritans and the Jews. She wanted the Truth regarding worship.

The Samaritans worshipped God on Mount Gerizim. Mount Gerizim was a place of blessing (Deuteronomy 11:29), but the Jews worshiped in Jerusalem at the Temple. Gerizim was important for religious ceremonies. This is where the Israelites would acknowledge the blessings for obeying God and the cursings of disobeying Him (Deuteronomy 27). The stones of memorial, an altar, were placed close by as a reminder of what God had done for them.

Jesus expounds on the reality of worship. *It's not about a place but a PERSON.*

Worship may, on occasion, happen in a church or public setting. But it should be an overflow of a continual occurrence in the private place of the worshiper's heart.

This worship connects the heart of the believer to the truth of God. The truth of God is revealed in the person of Jesus.

This is the best part. Jesus breaks down the prejudice and spiritual barrier and shows her need for salvation. Not just for the Jews. Not just for the Samaritans. But for the entire world. Jesus reveals Himself to her as the MESSIAH.

She is stunned by this statement, and her response is amazing. She left her water pot. This was the reminder of her former self. This was the baggage of her past decisions that she continued to carry. She left it all behind. This happens when we have an encounter with Jesus. Now she is running towards the city.

Study Questions

1. She was utterly shocked when Jesus responded to her in vs. 26 *"Jesus saith unto her, I that speak unto thee am he."* Jesus gave her the TRUTH that would eternally change the trajectory of her life. He is the Messiah that everyone was looking for. He was Christ, the Savior of the world. Jesus changes everything. Read Psalm 86. List at least five things that you can worship the Lord for. How do these things directly affect or change you?

2. Do you ever struggle with misplaced worship? Do you try to fill in the holes of your heart with temporal things that only leave you lacking? We should join with all the earth in singing praises of worship to God. Read Psalm 148 and write out verse 13. Take time to write down a few things you are devoting more time and energy to than your relationship with the Lord. These things may not always be sinful, but they can become idols when we give them more attention than they deserve. God alone is worthy of our praise and worship.

3. The word "worthy" in our dictionary means "having worth or value." The word "worship" means "an act of adoration, reverence, and devotion." Jesus is worth our worship. Read Revelation 5 and write out verse 12. How does this chapter change your perspective on your worship of Jesus? Meditate on that chapter. Reread it several times. Which verses stand out most to you and why?

Daily Study - Day 4
Read John 4:27, 31-38

"Tell me, and I forget. Teach me, and I remember. Involve me, and I learn." –
Benjamin Franklin.

The greatest life lessons are concreted in our minds because it was more than a passing statement, but an action played out before our eyes.

The disciples returned to where they left Jesus and must have been completely shocked. Jesus was sitting at the well, speaking with a woman. A Samaritan woman. This would have been a little unsettling for these men, but they didn't say a word. They just watched.

The woman returns to the city out of pure joy and excitement to share the Good News.

Meanwhile, the disciples were back at the well and were concerned for Jesus and His physical needs. They wanted Jesus to eat and be filled and comfortable. Jesus gave a gentle reminder that His "meat" was to do God's will. Jesus wasn't looking for physical comfort, but spiritual comfort that delights the soul. This delight was fulfilling the will of His Father. They couldn't understand the spiritual work Jesus was doing. They were having a hard time being concerned for this woman's spiritual needs because they were not seeing her as Jesus saw her. They didn't understand the finishing work of Jesus.

We see this completed work explained in Jesus's prayer in John 17.

John 1:1-4 [Read John 1]
"These words spake Jesus, and lifted up his eyes to heaven, and said, Father, the hour is come; glorify thy Son, that thy Son also may glorify thee: as thou hast given him power over all flesh, that he should give eternal life to as many as thou hast given him. And this is life eternal, that they might know thee the only true God, and Jesus Christ, whom thou has sent. I have glorified thee on earth: I have finished the work which thou hast gavest me to do."

Jesus wanted to do God's will. He wanted to show salvation to all men. He wanted the disciples to understand what God's will was for them - to see everyone's need for salvation through Jesus.

OPEN YOUR EYES AND SEE THE HARVEST.

God's will is not down the road. It's not something that will eventually come. It is here and now. People need the Lord.

We need to be going after people. We must stop allowing things that make us uncomfortable and hinder us from giving the Gospel to everybody. The work needs to be done now.

We see the teaching moment here, which is solidified in Matthew 9.

Matthew 9:36-37
"But when he saw the multitudes, he was moved with compassion on them, because they fainted, and were scattered abroad, as sheep having no shepherd. Then saith he unto his disciples, The harvest truly is plenteous, but the labourers are few, Pray ye therefore the Lord of the harvest, that he will send forth labourers into his harvest."

Did you get that? Jesus has a prayer request for laborers. The need and work of the harvest are great. Jesus saw the multitude of people, and it stirred compassion in His heart.

Do you see people and allow the Holy Spirit to stir compassion in your heart?

Does your compassion drive you to be consistent in praying for laborers?

Does your prayer for laborers encourage you to be an active laborer?

It took the disciple's involvement to grasp this great need and command fully.

This is God's will for His people to do His work.

"Miracles follow the plow." – A.W. Tozer

Study Questions

1. Compassion is a mixed passion combined with love and sorrow. Jesus saw people and had compassion. He saw their physical and spiritual needs and desired to meet those needs. We read where Jesus miraculously fed thousands, healed many, and desired to save all. When was the last time you saw a person who had a physical need, and you allowed your compassion to interchange with an action? Write about this instance and allow it to launch you to do more.

2. When was the last time you saw someone in need spiritually, and you chose to meet that need (a need for salvation, a need for encouragement, a need for prayer)? Pray and ask God to open your eyes to see the harvest. Ask Him to give you a heart of compassion and not just allow it to move you to pray for laborers, but to motivate you to be a laborer. Write at least three or more names that God impresses on your heart to sow spiritually in their lives.

3. Read Jude and write out verse 22. How does this chapter challenge you to do the work God has called us to do? This book reminds Christians that we have faith to contend for and a common salvation that needs to be delivered. Certain men have crept in unnoticed, distracting and taking away from the work God has called us to do. Remember the words of Jesus and keep building, keep praying and keep loving.

Daily Study - Day 5
Read John 4:28-30, 39-43

Words are powerful. The Bible gives us so much wisdom and warnings on the subject.

Proverbs 18:21
"Death and life are in the power of the tongue: And they that love it shall eat the fruit thereof."

What you say matters. Make your words count. This is precisely what the Samaritan woman does here. She understands Whom she is talking to; and wants to tell everyone what she has discovered. She wasn't willing to keep Jesus a secret. She believed on Him and wanted others to have this Living Water.

Romans 10:11
"For the scripture saith, Whosoever believeth on him shall not be ashamed."

She was no longer ashamed. What a miracle. Her shame melted away when she met the Savior. She now had a boldness to run and speak to others about this great salvation. Her brokenness was made beautiful.

Romans 10:13-15
"For whosoever shall call upon the name of the Lord shall be saved. How then shall they call on whom they have not believed? and how shall they believe on whom they have not heard? and how shall they hear without a preacher? and how shall they preach, except they be sent? as it is written, How beautiful are the feet of them that preach the gospel of peace, and bring glad tidings of good things!"

Don't be fooled by these verses, ladies. The word preacher here has the meaning of "one who proclaims." We are all to be proclaiming the Gospel of Jesus. It's not just your pastor's job. It's not the evangelist's job. It is not the Sunday School teacher's job. It's every Christian's job. IT IS YOUR JOB!

This woman's life became a beautiful testimony to the redeeming grace of Jesus. Yours can be, too. No one is too far gone for the Lord to redeem and restore.

Many Samaritans believed on Jesus because of the words of this woman. Her people came to the well to hear Him for themselves. They begged Jesus to stay with them for a couple of days, and He agreed.

Many more Samaritans believed because of the words of Jesus. Our words are important, but nothing is better than God's Word. When Jesus spoke, something spectacular happened. The Samaritans were brought to Jesus by this woman, and they believed because they heard His words. They trusted that Jesus was the Messiah, the Savior of the world.

Have others come to know Jesus because of your words?

The testimony we have is powerful when we allow God to use it.

Revelation 12:10-12
"And I heard a loud voice saying in heaven, Now is come salvation, and strength, and the kingdom of our God, and the power of his Christ: for the accuser of our brethren is cast down, which accused them before God day and night. And they overcame him by the blood of the Lamb, and by the word of their testimony: and they loved not their lives unto the death. Therefore rejoice, ye heavens, and ye that dwell in them...for the devil is come down unto you, having great wrath, because he knoweth that he hath but a short time."

It's not our words alone. It's our words partnered with the only Word that matters...God's Word. The power comes from the blood of the Lamb. The power is in salvation, and salvation only comes through Jesus.

Acts 4:10, 12
"Be it known unto you all, and to all the people of Israel, that by the name of Jesus Christ of Nazareth, whom ye crucified, whom God raised from the dead, even by him doth this man stand here before you whole... Neither is there salvation in any other: for there is none other name under heaven given among men, whereby we must be saved."

The Gospel is the miraculous, virgin birth of Jesus. The perfect, sinless life of Jesus. He willingly and sacrificially went to the cross for your sin, my sin, and the whole world's sins. He conquered death and the grave when He triumphantly rose again. He ascended into heaven and now sits on the right hand of God, interceding for the saints. Do you believe?

Study Questions

1. Do you use your words wisely? Read Psalm 19:14 and write it out. Use this verse as an exposure of your heart. The Bible tells us in Luke 6:45, *"A good man out of the good treasure of his heart bringeth forth that which is good, and an evil man out of the evil treasure of his heart bringeth forth that which is evil: for of the abundance of the heart his mouth speaketh."* Your words reflect your heart. Does your heart belong to the Lord?

2. You may feel like your life isn't capable of making an impact. God can use anything that is wholly surrendered to Him. Look at the results of this woman's testimony of transformation. Read Acts 8:1-17. What transpired in this passage because of the Samaritan Woman's encounter with Jesus?

3. This woman's story should convict our hearts to do more for the Gospel's sake. What about this account has stirred you to believe in Jesus and witness for Him? James 1:22-24, *"But be ye doers of the word, and not hearers only, deceiving your own selves. For if any man be a hearer of the word, and not a doer, he is like unto a man beholding his natural face in a glass: For he beholdeth himself, and goeth his way, and straightway forgetteth what manner of man he was."* What practical actions will you take that will express this stirring?

Priscilla and Aquila
Helpers in Christ

ENCOURAGEMENT FROM WOMEN

Week 6 - Video Session Notes
Priscilla and Aquila: Helpers in Christ

Introduction:

_____

_____

_____

_____

I.   Helpers _____ **their Hardships**

Greet Priscilla and Aquila my helpers in Christ Jesus. Romans 16:3

II.   _____ Serving

Greet Priscilla and Aquila my helpers in Christ Jesus: who have for my life laid down their own necks: unto whom not only I give thanks, but also all the churches of the Gentiles. Likewise greet the church that is in their house. Romans 16:3-5

Priscilla is part of a dynamic duo, one half of an amazing married couple that Paul met on one of his missionary journeys. A package deal, this couple is always mentioned in Scripture together. Side by side, their influence into the lives of Paul, Apollos, and the early church is a wonderful example of true Helpers in Christ.

III.   Encouraged Others in _____ **Matters**

The churches of Asia salute you. Aquila and Priscilla salute you much in the Lord, with the church that is in their house. 1 Corinthians 16:19

Salute Priscilla and Aquila, and the household of Onesiphorus. 2 Timothy 4:19

Working behind the scenes, Priscilla and Aquila exemplified what it meant to be part of the body of Christ. Together as one flesh, they faithfully served as helpers to Paul and the early church. They were united with a common purpose and their lives brought glory to God. A friendship that spanned twenty years, a bond that was created while ministering together and working to further the gospel of Christ; Priscilla, Aquila and Paul, though miles apart, experienced a closeness that comes from serving God together.

Conclusion:

_____

_____

_____

_____

Answers: *Despite, Actively, Spiritual*

Daily Study - Day 1

Helpers Despite hardship.

The apostle Paul had been traveling and preaching throughout cities like Philippi, Thessalonica and Athens. He had seen miracles of prison doors opening, people receiving the word with all readiness of mind, and he had just finished preaching a powerful sermon at Mar's hill. After all of this Paul comes to Corinth, a narrow stretch of land which is located in South-central Greece. There he meets a married couple, Aquila and Priscilla, working together making tents at a local farmer's market.

Acts 18:2, *And found a certain Jew named Aquila, born in Pontus, lately come from Italy, with his wife Priscilla; (because that Claudius had commanded all Jews to depart from Rome:) and came unto them.*

Priscilla and Aquila had to go through some difficult trials before they came to a place where they could be effective helpers in Christ. Because of Emperor Claudius expelling the Jews from Rome, many Jews were uprooted from their homes, including Priscilla and Aquila. This brought them to Corinth where they set up shop making tents. There are not many details given but it doesn't take much of an imagination to know how hard this must have been. Leaving their homes, their families and the world they knew had to have been traumatic and emotional.

As the reader of the stories in the Bible, we have the vantage point of getting to read the end of the stories and see how God works and how God brings people through difficulties. When Priscilla and Aquila were going through the persecution and exile of the Jews, they didn't know how their story would end or how God would use them. They had to continue by faith. It may have been a coincidence that they met Paul at the market place, but I think it was more of a divine appointment.

"You make tents! I make tents!"
"You love Jesus! I love Jesus!"
"Wanna stay at our place while you share the good news?"
"You can work with us, too!"
"Awesome!"

Acts 18:3 *And because he was of the same craft, he abode with them, and wrought: for by their occupation they were tent makers.*

In Paul's letter to the Corinthians, he reveals to the reader how he came to Corinth. He says, "I was with you in weakness, and in fear". When they meet there seems to be an instant connection. God knew that Priscilla and Aquila could be a help to Paul and that Paul could be a help to them. They became co-laborers together, not just in tent-making, but in furthering the gospel.

1 Corinthians 2:3, *And I was with you in weakness, and in fear, and in much trembling.*

They may have connected over tent-making, but what bonded them was their common purpose, which was Jesus. Priscilla and Aquila could have never planned this encounter or envisioned the roll they would play as intricate members of the early church. Had they not have been exiled from Rome, had they not have moved to Corinth, had they not have been making tents at that certain moment in time on that day, the story could have been very different. God had a plan and purpose for this faithful couple.

The trials and tribulations that brought Priscilla, Aquila and Paul to this moment in the market place was part of a greater story. Our stories are no different. What if God is bringing us through some hardships and difficult moments to bring us to a place where we can be a more effective helper in Christ? He had a plan for Aquila and Priscilla and they were greatly used, and God also has a plan for each and every one of us. We can trust the words of Paul in Romans 8:28, *And we know that all things work together for good to them that love God, to them who are the called according to his purpose.*

God is ordering our steps, he is directing our paths, we are not alone, and he has a plan for our lives. We are in the middle of our stories. What we can learn from Priscilla and Aquila is that God had a purpose for their life, and the ripple effect of their influence would affect eternity. As we continue to trust God through life, we too have a purpose that can affect eternity.

Psalm 37:23, *The steps of a good man are ordered by the Lord: and he delighteth in his way.*

Study Questions

1. What brought Priscilla and Aquila to Corinth?

2. How were Aquila and Priscilla a blessing to Paul?

3. Connect the dots of a difficult moment in your life to show how God worked.

Daily Study - Day 2

Helpers in their Home.

Acts 18:3, 11, *And because he was of the same craft, he abode with them, and wrought: for by their occupation they were tentmakers. And he continued there a year and six months teaching the word of God among them.*

Priscilla and Aquila had a home that they used for the glory of God. First, they gave Paul a place to stay while he continued sharing Christ within the synagogues and community. For a year and a half, Paul lived with them. What a blessing it must have been for Paul, a traveling evangelist, to have a steady place to stay and sleep. Eventually they used their home to host churches, not only in Corinth, but in Ephesus, and in Rome.

Their home provided a resting place for Paul and a place of learning for the new believer. The early church relied on people's homes to have a place to meet. Priscilla and Aquila met that need more than once. It would not surprise me that when Paul's fellow missionary buddies came to town that they also stayed with Aquila and Priscilla. They were a great example of hospitality.

Hospitality: "The act or practice of receiving and entertaining strangers or guests without reward, or with kind and generous liberality."

When Paul sailed to Syria and Aquila and Priscilla sailed with him to help continue sharing the Gospel, they once again left their home, but this time it was their choice. Their home had become a tool that they used to help facilitate ministry, and they were not so tied to their earthly home that it kept them from ministering elsewhere. The security of an eternal home in heaven gives us a perspective that is heavenly minded and not earthly-minded.

In Paul's letter to the Romans and the Corinthians, he acknowledges the churches that are meeting in Priscilla and Aquila's house. This may give new understanding to the term, "The house of God." As Paul, Apollos, the disciples, and faithful followers of Christ continued to spread the amazing grace of Jesus Christ, homes were needed for gatherings. Without a house to meet in, the new believers would not have a place to grow in their faith and be discipled. Homes were important to the growth of the church, and those who hosted the church in their homes were faithful facilitators.

Homes are still necessary for the growth of the church. We need willing servants to open their homes and gather together in fellowships, Bible studies, and ministry. The example of Priscilla and Aquila using their earthly home for an eternal purpose should challenge us to use our homes to honor God.

1 Corinthians 16:19 *The churches of Asia salute you. Aquila and Priscilla salute you much in the Lord, with the church that is in their house.*

Romans 16:5a *Likewise greet the church that is in their house.*

Acts 18:5 *And when Silas and Timotheus were come from Macedonia Paul was pressed in the spirit, and testified to the Jews that Jesus was Christ.*

1 Peter 4:8-10 *And above all things have fervent charity among yourselves: for charity shall cover the multitude of sins. Use hospitality one to another without grudging. As every man hath received the gift, even so minister the same one to another, as good stewards of the manifold grace of God.*

Study Questions

1. How did Priscilla and Aquila use their home to minister?

2. When was a time that someone opened their home and ministered to you? How did that help you?

3. In what way can you use your home more effectively to serve the Lord?

4. What keeps us less tied to our home here on earth?

Daily Study - Day 3

Helpers in Helping.

Acts 18:18-19, *And Paul after this tarried there yet a good while, and then took his leave of the brethren, and sailed thence into Syria, and with him Priscilla and Aquila; having shorn his head in Cenchrea: for he had a vow. And he came to Ephesus, and left them there: but he himself entered into the synagogue, and reasoned with the Jews.*

Psalm 54:4, *Behold, God is my helper: The Lord is with them that uphold my soul.*

Hebrews 13:6, *So that we may boldly say, The Lord is my helper, and I will not fear what man shall do unto me.*

Many times, throughout Scripture, God is called a "helper." Maybe: Being called a helper brings honor to the position of helper. God put us on earth to be helpers in Christ, to love God, and to love people, and to help further the message of redeeming grace through Jesus Christ. Priscilla and Aquila fulfilled an indispensable roll in the ministry of Paul and the early church. More importantly, they lived out what it means to be a Christian by being Christ-like in their ministry of helping.

Practically, Priscilla and Aquila helped in providing Paul a place to stay, a place to work, a home to meet in and partners to travel with. They were a team whose ultimate goal was reaching the lost. When Paul needed them to stay in Ephesus, they did just that. Whether it was using their home, traveling, or taking in young preachers, the willingness of this couple is a wonderful picture of what it means to be a helper in Christ.

The blessing of serving and being a helper in Christ is the front row seat to the workings of the Holy Spirit. The City of Corinth, the "Sin City" of its day, was being evangelized. More and more people were believing and getting baptized, and Priscilla and Aquila were there, part of that wonderful story. For a year and a half, they witnessed the power of God working in Corinth through Paul. After Corinth, they once again saw God move in Ephesus as they helped Apollos and used their house as a home church. From there it was Rome and the church that Paul greeted that was meeting in their house. Their faithful, willing involvement and active serving throughout their lives is an incredible testimony. To be God's helper is an honor and blessed achievement of eternal impact.

Study Questions

1. List all the ways Priscilla and Aquila were helpers in Acts 18, Romans 16:3-5, and 1 Corinthians 16:19.

2. What is the blessing of serving and being a helper in Christ?

3. What are some practical ways you can be a help in your home, church, and community?

Daily Study – Day 4

Helpers in Holy Happenings.

What a privilege it must have been for Aquila and Priscilla to have Paul in their home, to have a front row seat to his ministry, and to be able to learn and grow under him. Oh, to be a fly on the wall listening to those late evening discussions that Aquila, Priscilla and Paul must have had over a cup of hot tea while discussing doctrine, and ministry, and dreams of furthering the Gospel to the world. Who knows what they talked about, but when you live with one of the greatest Apostles and teachers of that generation, you would think some deep spiritual conversations must have happened.

Their time learning and growing with Paul in Corinth, gave Priscilla and Aquila a strong foundation in the doctrines of the Gospel, and prepared them for the next step in their ministry. When they traveled with Paul to Syria, and left Ephesus, that is where they met Apollos. Apollos was a gifted orator of God's Word, but his knowledge of Christ, the Gospel, and the Holy Spirit was limited. It was here that this faithful couple took the time to more perfectly expound unto Apollos the way of God.

Acts 18:26, And he began to speak boldly in the synagogue: whom when Aquila and Priscilla had heard, they took him unto them, and expounded unto him the way of God more perfectly.

Both Priscilla and Aquila took the time to encourage and direct Apollos in spiritual matters together. They knew what they believed and they discipled Apollos. This young preacher then went on to be greatly used by God in helping to further declare the gospel in Corinth and beyond. Some even believe he could be the author of the book of Hebrews. What an incredible help this couple was in directing Apollos.

When we know God, desire to study the Scriptures, and become students of the Word, we too can be a blessing in helping to direct others in spiritual matters. Priscilla and Aquila were just your average married couple who worked full-time, yet the influence they had in the early church was magnificent. Their willing spirit to go with Paul, stay in Ephesus when Paul asked them, and spend time with Apollos to help him understand foundational doctrines, should be praised. Not everyone is called to be a missionary or pastor, but we are all called to share the love of God.

Study Questions

1. How did Priscilla and Aquila use their spiritual knowledge to be a help?

2. Why is it important to be a student of Scripture and know what you believe?

3. In what ways can you use your knowledge of God to encourage others in Christ?

Daily Study – Day 5

Helpers in Heart.

2 Timothy 4:19, Salute Prisca and Aquila, and the household of Onesiphorus.

In Paul's last letter to Timothy, he once again greets his friends but this time he uses Priscilla's shortened name, or nickname maybe. Whatever it was it just seems a bit more endearing; like how an old friend may have a unique or special way of saying your name. Serving God together unites our hearts.

As Paul was writing his letters, and maybe reminiscing and thinking about all those he crossed paths with, and worked with over the course of his ministry, I'm sure he was filled with gratitude and love. His heart was bonded to this amazing couple he met twenty or so years earlier, and by greeting them he wanted them to know they were thought of. It can almost bring you to tears when you think about all that must have been going through Paul' mind. He was stuck in this prison. Not to mention the impending death at the hand of Nero. He was not able to see those whom he was closest to. I imagine him trying to make sure all the churches had letters with the last bits of wisdom he had for them. This must have been a bit overwhelming. We know God was orchestrating this all, but for a moment empathize with Paul.

When Priscilla and Aquila opened their home to Paul, they got so much more than just a roommate. God opened doors of friendship, ministry, led them to places where they were used to help the cause of Christ, and knit their hearts to those they served with, like Paul. Because of their willing spirit, the impact that Priscilla and Aquila had on the early church was exponential.

We truly are closest to those with whom we serve. As comrades in Christ, when you are serving, praying, and in the proverbial trenches of ministry together, there is a closeness that knits your hearts together. In the way Paul addresses his friends, not only can you can see that Priscilla and Aquila had become faithful kindred spirits to Paul, but that Paul was thankful for friends willing to sacrifice their lives for his.

Romans 16: 3-4, Greet Priscilla and Aquila my helpers in Christ Jesus: Who have for my life laid down their own necks: unto whom not only I give thanks, but also all the churches of the Gentiles.

John 15:13, Greater love hath no man that this, that a man lay down his life for his friends.

Priscilla and her husband Aquila are true couple goals. More than that it should be the goal of every believer to live a life of willingness to be a helper in Christ. We have learned that despite their hardships, they became servants, graciously using their home wherever God directed them, and becoming faithful church planters with Paul. Serving the Lord together, side-by-side, and nurturing faith in others, shows us what God can accomplish through simply being active followers of God. May we be challenged by the example of Priscilla and Aquila and their role of being helpers in Christ.

Study Questions

1. Why was Paul thankful to Priscilla and Aquila?

2. What spiritual contribution are you making into the lives of others?

3. Think about those who are helpers in Christ to you, your Priscilla and Aquila. Write them a note this week to thank them for their encouragement and help in your life.

Encouragement From Women
(EFW)

EFW seeks to provide biblical encouragement for women around the globe through social media, ladies devotional books, online webinars, and podcasts. Visit encouragementfromwomen.com to sign up for upcoming events, view our latest resource, and read the latest blog.

Encouragement From Women
Devotionals

Encouragement from Women devotional books are the perfect gift! *Encouragement for Women, Encouragement for Your Identity, Encouragement for Motherhood,* and *Encouragement for Little Women.* Visit Amazon to order yours today!

You Can Know You're Going to Heaven!

The most encouraging thing we can learn from Bible study is knowing that we can have an eternal home in Heaven! Bible study is amazing! The most important thing we can study in Scripture is the Gospel. What is the Gospel? It's the good news of Jesus Christ! The good news that Jesus is God, that He loves us, that He became a man, that He lived a perfect life, and that He gave His perfect self for us by dying on a cross. The good news doesn't end there. Jesus proved that He is God by raising Himself from the dead! If we place our faith in Him for the forgiveness of our sins, we can spend eternity with Him. That, my friend, is the good new of Jesus!

Scripture states, *Moreover, brethren, I declare unto you the gospel which I preached unto you, which also ye have received, and wherein ye stand... how that Christ died for our sins according to the scriptures; And that he was buried, and that he rose again the third day according to the scriptures.* - 1 Corinthians 15:1-4

Jesus cares so much for us. In fact, He cared about us so much that 2,000 years ago, He left the glory of Heaven to come to earth so that He could give us the gift of eternal life in His eternal home. The question is, how can we get this gift?

Have you ever told a lie, lost your temper, or taken something that didn't belong to you? We all have. The Bible calls the breaking of God's law – sin.
For all have sinned, and come short of the glory of God. – Romans 3:23

Our sin separates us from God, and must be paid for. *For the wages of sin is death: but the gift of God is eternal life through Jesus Christ our Lord.* – Romans 6:23

Now for the good news…Jesus Christ willingly was crucified, buried, and rose from the dead in order to pay for our sins. *Christ died for our sins according to the scriptures; And that he was buried, and that he rose again the third day according to the scriptures.* – 1 Corinthians 15:3-4

God allowed this because He is actively pursuing our hearts. *But God commendeth his love toward us, in that, while we were yet sinners, Christ died for us.* – Romans 5:8

Jesus offers us an eternal home in Heaven if we simply believe on Him for salvation. We confirm this belief by calling on Him. *That if thou shalt confess with thy mouth the Lord Jesus, and shalt believe in thine heart that God hath raised him from the dead, thou shalt be saved...For whosoever shall call upon the name of the Lord shall be saved.* – Romans 10:9, 13

If you've placed your trust in Christ after reading this you are officially part of the family of God! You may have questions and we would love to answer them! Please contact us so we can celebrate with you!

Welcome to the family!

Notes / Prayer Requests

Notes / Prayer Requests

Made in the USA
Columbia, SC
31 January 2023

11310374R00061